VIRGO

James Petulengro

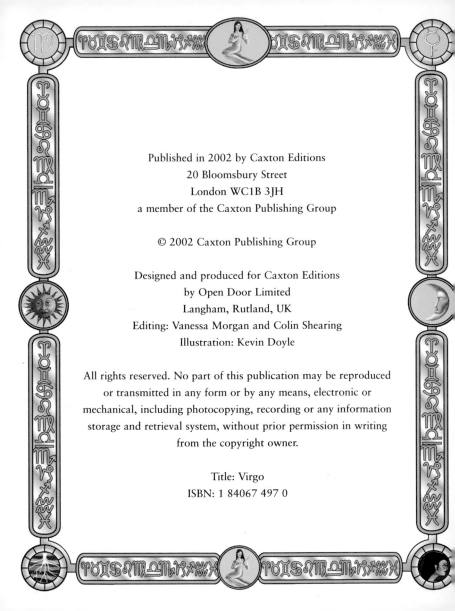

Published in 2002 by Caxton Editions
20 Bloomsbury Street
London WC1B 3JH
a member of the Caxton Publishing Group

© 2002 Caxton Publishing Group

Designed and produced for Caxton Editions
by Open Door Limited
Langham, Rutland, UK
Editing: Vanessa Morgan and Colin Shearing
Illustration: Kevin Doyle

Title: Virgo
ISBN: 1 84067 497 0

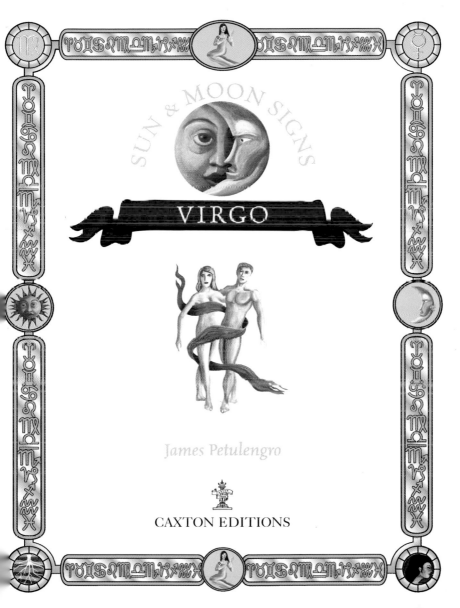

SUN & MOON SIGNS

VIRGO

James Petulengro

CAXTON EDITIONS

VIRGO
CONTENTS

VIRGO
CONTENTS

VIRGO
INTRODUCTION

The art and science of astrology has been around for over 5,000 years
and is still used by many people for many different purposes. The
scientific aspect of the subject is in the astronomical calculations required to
make a birth chart. A birth chart (horoscope) is like a photographic
image of the planets in the sky above you when you are born. No two
people in the world have the same birth chart; it is totally unique to you
and is what defines your individuality. You may have many things in
common with other people, but the complete birth chart is yours and yours
alone. The artistic aspect of the subject is in the interpretation of the
position of these planetary bodies. In this book we shall be looking
particularly at the positions of the Sun and the Moon at the time of your
birth and how these affect your life.

Introduction

You may find that if you were born from the 19th to the 23rd of the month your Sun sign is what is called "on the cusp". Each year the Sun enters the various Sun signs on different days so just because you were born on the 21st of the month, for example, does not necessarily mean you are the Sun sign you think you are. Calculating your birth chart will help you to discover exactly what your Sun sign is.

As a special feature, if you do not have one already, you can calculate your own birth chart including a short 8-page interpretation on my website at http://www.jamespetulengro.co.uk type in your birth details and you can then print out astrological details and your birth chart. This may also help you when you come to look at the Moon sign part of this book and the Sun and Moon combinations if you do not know your Moon sign.

Introduction

The 12 Zodiac signs are traditionally formed in four groups within which they interact and complement each other.

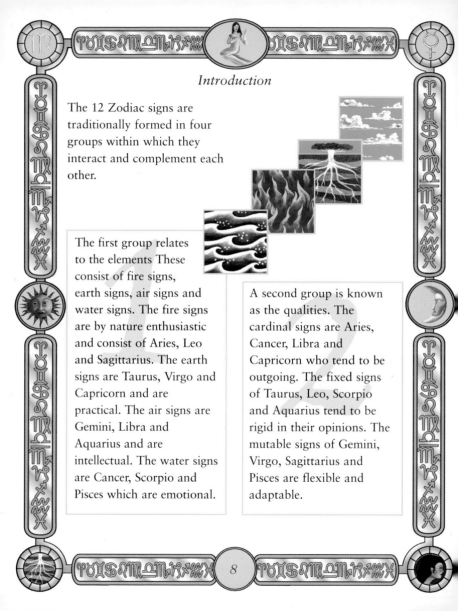

The first group relates to the elements These consist of fire signs, earth signs, air signs and water signs. The fire signs are by nature enthusiastic and consist of Aries, Leo and Sagittarius. The earth signs are Taurus, Virgo and Capricorn and are practical. The air signs are Gemini, Libra and Aquarius and are intellectual. The water signs are Cancer, Scorpio and Pisces which are emotional.

A second group is known as the qualities. The cardinal signs are Aries, Cancer, Libra and Capricorn who tend to be outgoing. The fixed signs of Taurus, Leo, Scorpio and Aquarius tend to be rigid in their opinions. The mutable signs of Gemini, Virgo, Sagittarius and Pisces are flexible and adaptable.

Introduction

The third group refers to positivity/masculinity and negativity/femininity. The positive signs are Aries, Gemini, Leo, Libra, Sagittarius and Aquarius. These people tend to be extroverts. The negative/feminine signs are Taurus, Cancer, Virgo, Scorpio, Capricorn and Pisces and these signs tend to be introverts. Do not be confused if you are a Virgo man as this does not mean that you lack masculinity any more than a woman with a masculine Sun sign lacks femininity, although Virgo is regarded as one of the female signs.

Lastly the fourth group is known as the polarities. This indicates the special relationship a sign has with its polar opposite. Polar signs complement each other so that there is a special rapport and understanding between them. For example, as Virgo is one of the most practical of signs, Pisces, its polar opposite, is the most dreamy of the Zodiac signs. Ruling planets – each sign is ruled by one of the planets, each planet has a very similar energy to the sign it rules. For example, Virgo is ruled by Mercury, the messenger god, who carries the caduceus, the staff of healing.

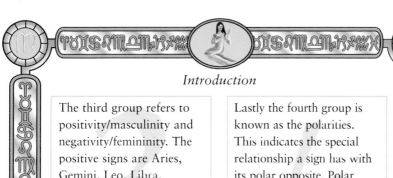

SUN SIGNS
WHAT ARE THEY?

The Sun is the star at the centre of our solar system which is composed of nine planets. The Earth is the third one out, at a distance of 93 million miles. The Sun is 109 times the size of the Earth and without it there would be no life. It is the most powerful of all the bodies in our solar system and exerts a gravitational pull upon all of us. It affects each of our personalities so strongly that a person who is born under a particular sign will continue to have those characteristics throughout their life. The Sun is the fuel of our solar system, just as the Sun is the fuel of your personality.

Your Sun sign, or sign of the Zodiac, depends on the month of the year that you were born in because the Earth travels around the Sun once in approximately 365 days and the Sun appears to travel through one of 12 constellations in the sky above.

Sun Signs – What are They?

Looking at your Sun sign should not be confused with studying the daily horoscopes that you will find in magazines or newspapers. In this book we are examining the effect that your Sun sign has on your personality rather than predictions. You were born between 21st August to 21st September which makes you a Virgo.

Some astrologers feel that Sun sign readings are too much of a generalisation, as if all butchers, bakers and candlestick makers were the same. However, the Sun, as I said earlier, is the most powerful body in our whole life and that reflects in the accuracy of Sun sign readings.

If you know someone's Sun sign you are most certainly much more informed about that person than not knowing it.

Your Sun sign personality is the personality that you present to people because it is what you cherish and is what you are most proud of about yourself. To be more specific the placement of your Sun sign represents how you express your ego. In general a person's Sun sign will represent how they present themselves to the world during daylight hours and their Moon sign will represent how they present themselves as dusk arrives and their more intimate, hidden side comes out.

MOON SIGNS
WHAT ARE THEY?

The Moon is the Earth's satellite and is, approximately 250,000 miles away. Although only small in diameter, 2,160 miles, the Moon exerts considerable gravitational influence on the Earth and is responsible for the tides. It orbits the Earth in approximately 28 days, known as the lunar cycle, and passes through each sign of the Zodiac every 2.5 days. In your birth chart it is considered almost as important as the Sun, but its influences are different. The Moon holds sway over your moods and emotional life. Whereas the Sun is your day, the Moon represents your night.

Your Moon sign represents how you deal with and express your tender, caring side and your emotional responses in general. It represents your instinctive, unconscious, primitive, habitual personality. How you express yourself is affected by your Moon sign. It represents

Moon Signs – What are They?

your basic emotional needs and how you interact with others. It represents your gut instinct and how you react to things when you are caught by surprise, particularly when you feel you are threatened. Another important area that the Moon controls is that of your domestic arena. Since it is the planet that rules Cancer, the Moon is seen as feminine, watery, negative and reflective.

Some people do have the same sign for the Sun and the Moon, so both their ego and emotions are ruled by the same sign. This will generally provide a pattern of consistency through many situations in your life.

Above: your Moon sign represents your basic emotional needs and how you interact with others.

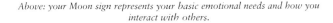

VIRGO
THE SUN SIGN

If you are a Virgo and if we met and I began to explain to you your personality through your horoscope, you would concentrate hard on every part of what I said, down to the finest detail, because Virgoans love to analyse more than anything else. You may also be over-critical and concerned about the scientific basis of my observations.

Virgo

21st August to 21st September

Positive Traits

Practical, analytical, intelligent, meticulous, reliable, modest

Negative Traits

Fussy, over-critical, worrying, harsh, nagging

Traditional Associations

Zodiac Symbol: The Virgin
Glyph: ♍
Ruling Planet: Mercury
Ruling House: The Sixth
Gender: Feminine and Negative
Polarity: Pisces
Element: Earth
Quality: Mutable
Key Phrase: I Analyse
Body Area: The Stomach, the Intestines and the Nervous System
Colour: Pale Green
Metal: Nickel
Gemstone: Sardonyx and Blue Lace Agate
Foods: Carrots, potatoes, blackberries, celeriac, sage, almonds, pomegranate
Flora: Cornflower, lavender, grapevine, privet, wintergreen, white poplar, hazel, apple

Virgo – the Sun Sign

Countries: *Turkey, Brazil, Greece, Crete, Jordan, West Indies*
Cities: *Athens, Lyons, Boston, Paris, Corinth*
Tarot Card: *The Hermit*
Deities: *Ceres, Demeter and Virgin Mary*
Activity: *Nutrition*

Virgo is earthy and ruled by the planet Mercury, named after the Roman messenger god. Since it is a mutable sign and ruled by the negative aspect of Mercury, Virgoans are intellectual yet concerned with the practicality of their mental processes. They are natural worriers. This is also the most modest of all the signs.

As the sixth sign, Virgo represents the early autumn, the harvest and productivity.

They are represented by the Virgin and, accordingly, the Virgoan has the most purity of intention of the signs. The planet Mercury is considered to govern the intellect, so the mind of the Virgoan is clear and analytical.

Virgoans are gentle. They are unlikely to be found at wild parties because they are invariably working late. They usually have a problem on their mind that they are trying to solve. Worry comes naturally to them; indeed, many of them are even attached to the habit of worrying. If they have not got a problem, they will go and seek one. Problem-solving is their forte.

Virgo – the Sun Sign

They are unquestionably sincere and dependable, cool and capable and able to work intensely over long periods of time, even more so than the tougher, brawnier signs. Unfortunately, Virgos are capable of overdoing their mental machinations which can often lead to nervous breakdowns. They usually take on more work than they can manage and often strain themselves to breaking point in order to fulfil their work obligations. However, they are quite calm and calculating and their intricate and delicate mental mechanisms run smoothly.

Above: Virgoans usually take on more work than they can manage and often strain themselves to breaking point in order to fulfil their work obligations.

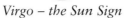

Virgo – the Sun Sign

They are fastidious in all things, particularly grooming and eating. Some overdo physical hygiene, though, to the point of showering four or five times a day. They dress meticulously, carefully picking out what they are going to wear that is appropriate to the situation.

With food, Virgoans are very fussy about what they eat; many of them are on diets or are health fanatics. They also rarely leave anything on the plate and scrape it clean, placing the cutlery neatly, as to leave it otherwise would be untidy.

Above: Virgoans are very fussy about what they want to eat; many of them are on diets or are health fanatics.

Virgo – the Sun Sign

Not all Virgos are prissy, fussy and dogmatic. Many of them possess a brilliant mercurial wit. They often give the appearance of daydreaming, although their dreams are eminently practical. This may fool people, but in reality their logical minds are working away, like a computer.

To most Virgos, the computer is the greatest invention ever. It is so like them: logical, detached and full of useful information. However, they are perfectionists and will find fault with whatever computer they have, always thinking of better programming or software capability, which no doubt other Virgoans are working away at creating!

Virgoans are creatures of habit and are constantly developing new habits for themselves. It makes them feel secure.

They apply their critical faculties to everything. If there is a job to be done full of boring or repetitive detail then a Virgo will effectively handle it. Their mercurial mind cannot stand procrastination, neglected detail or confusion of purpose and they will often straighten things out before even being asked. If they do go to a party, they only go there to help the host clean up at the end. In fact, a Virgoan invited to anyone's home will be more interested in washing up than anything else.

Virgo – the Sun Sign

To be fair, Virgos are the first to criticise themselves, fully aware of their own faults and weaknesses, better than anyone else.

They are visibly restless and tend to pace about, projecting a sense of urgency, as if they are late. They hate to be behind schedule as there is always something they have to do. Virgoans spend a great deal of time on their telephone or mobile or, even better, on their laptop.

Above: to most Virgos, the computer is the greatest invention ever.

Virgo – the Sun Sign

They do not like to be obligated to anyone for any reason. They particularly fear dependence in old age and that is what they are saving towards. Once they feel financially secure, however, they will spend money more freely. They still look for bargains, though, and if they are not happy with a product they will most certainly return it to the shop for a refund. They love discounts but have no sympathy for beggars or wasters, particularly timewasters.

Although Virgoans can sometimes appear to be selfish, or even stingy, they often find the greatest satisfaction in life by serving others. Virgos like cats, birds and small helpless creatures. They also like truth, punctuality, economy and prudence. They dislike sentiment, dirt, vulgarity, sloppiness and idleness.

They have a deeply practical nature and are true individualists whose keen perceptions are clear of wishful thinking. Once a Virgo has learned to master life's complicated details, they have the talent of shaping their own destiny with more certainty than any other Sun sign.

They need to beware that pessimism does not overcome them; they often believe that good fortune is soon followed by a double dose of misfortune.

Virgo – the Sun Sign

The Virgoan's gentle soul always responds to the call of duty. Behind their serious demeanour is the alluring Virgin, with purity of thought and purpose.

Above: Virgos like cats, birds and small helpless creatures.

Virgo – the Sun Sign

YOUR BODY

Virgo people typically have a serious look on their face but usually have a delightful smile. They generally have a rather wiry build, and are quick-moving but with an air of nervous tension about them. Virgoans have unusually beautiful and peaceful eyes, which are so clear that reflections can be seen in them. They seem to sparkle with intelligence. The face of a Virgoan has a pure and tranquil expression, which belies their secret worrying. Most of them are highly attractive, with delicate noses, ears and lips yet there is sometimes a sharpness about their features. They are graceful and charming with slender necks.

They are always meticulous and conservative in their dress. Virgoans are normally daintily built but often have more strength than their fragile appearance would suggest. They are always clean and tidy and are usually quite shy and retiring.

Above: the face of a Virgoan has a pure and tranquil expression, which belies their secret worrying.

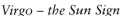

Virgo – the Sun Sign

YOUR POSSESSIONS

Virgos are rarely possessive but are often suspicious. As they are such pessimists they expect their possessions to go missing. Accordingly, they tend to be overly concerned with security and lock and hide everything away. Once they trust, however, they will share. They are also very careful about what they spend their money on and will spend hours analysing the pros and cons of any investment or even anything they might want to buy. They prefer to own new things as this means it is more likely to be clean and hygienic.

HOW YOU COMMUNICATE

Virgoans communicate carefully, analytically and critically. They plan ahead anything they may be doing, whether it is work or play. Even though their minds work very fast, they act slowly, taking everything into careful consideration along the way.

They are honest and plain-spoken people so rarely make good sales people. Indeed Virgoans may come across as abrupt and sharp-tongued. When they do communicate, it is done quietly and to the point. They prefer not to argue or create noise.

Virgo – the Sun Sign

YOUR HOME LIFE

Their homes, like the rest of their lives, are neat and tidy, even if they cannot see it for themselves. They are fastidious in their cleanliness and will spend a great deal of time working to make their home as perfect as possible. However, the Virgoan's vision of perfection is always just out of reach, no matter how much the place seems sparkling to everyone else.

Virgoans prefer clean, sharp lines and their homes are modern and usually minimalist in design. They like to use time-saving gadgets around the home. If the Virgoan is sharing their home, however tidy the other person believes him or herself to be, it will never be good enough for the Virgoan. Virgos also tend to worry about household bills and will have a comprehensive filing system designed to deal with them.

Above: Virgoans prefer clean, sharp lines and their homes are modern and usually minimalist in design.

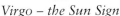

Virgo – the Sun Sign

YOUR CREATIVITY

When a Virgo does participate in anything creative, it has to have a practical end result. They are not the sort of person to starve in a bohemian bedsit, trying to create the world's best novel. Many of them do write because of the influence of their ruling planet Mercury. However, it is more likely to be of a journalistic nature where they can be sure to be paid for their work.

Virgoans need to have their children clean and tidy and will dress them in spotless clothes. All of their schedules, chores and school homework will be planned out carefully in advance. The children of a Virgoan are rarely able to live up to the high standards that a Virgoan parent sets for them. Virgos are usually firm disciplinarians with their children but never neglect them. They try to instil good habits but have a very tender and gentle touch so their children know they are loved. They are also very popular with children because they have a sense of humour that little ones can relate to.

Virgo – the Sun Sign

YOUR HEALTH

Many people believe that Virgoans are hypochondriacs, but it is not quite that simple. They are concerned about their health and love to discuss health issues. Virgoans are surprisingly healthy, although they usually carry their own pharmacy around with them. They tend to spend time researching any product that they might use. The words "organic", "pure" and "scientifically tested" appeal greatly to Virgos. They are always up to date on the latest health fad but are very discerning as to whether they believe it or not.

They have a tendency to suffer from upset stomachs, indigestion and chronic pains in the intestinal area. They are also susceptible to lung problems such as asthma, often of a nervous variety, and back aches. Many Virgoans are vegetarians, and even if they are not they know exactly what they should eat and how it should be cooked. They always make a point of washing their hands a great deal.

Virgo – the Sun Sign

Above: Virgoans are always up to date on the latest health fad but are very discerning as to whether they believe it or not.

 *Virgo – the Sun Sign*

YOUR RELATIONSHIPS

Virgos seek quality rather than quantity in romance. They have relatively few love affairs and many of them are disappointing. This has a lot to do with the Virgo's search for the perfect mate. They are one of the signs that can live easily with celibacy and, if fate decrees a single life for them, Virgo is prepared to accept it without emotional trauma. They are more likely to have a relationship with their work in which they can become deeply involved, even obsessively so.

However, when they do fall in love they do not make a song and dance about it. Strangely, when they want to be, they can be very seductive. Unfortunately, they often remain sufficiently detached to break a lot of hearts with their cool kind of flirting. Although they have many close friends, they rarely move friendship on from the platonic level.

Their modesty and fastidiousness prevent promiscuity. Virgos tend to remain technical virgins for their whole life because of their purity and outlook. There is always something clean and chaste about Virgoan love and they never allow it to become soiled. Lovemaking itself can be perhaps too undignified and unhygienic for them. They hold no illusions about love;

Virgo – the Sun Sign

they are looking for the real thing with the right person. They want decent, honest and genuine relationships. They also know how small a chance there is of them getting that but they will not compromise.

They are difficult to stir emotionally and hence they can go a long time without feeling any real passion or need for a permanent partner. Once they find that special someone, the Virgoan is the most faithful of all the signs.

Above: their modesty and fastidiousness prevent promiscuity. Virgos tend to remain technical virgins for their whole life because of their purity and outlook.

YOUR RESOURCES

Virgoans tend to be extremely frugal with their resources. Even though they may be earning a decent salary, achieved through hard work, they tend to be careful in the way they spend it. Rather than splash out on frivolities the Virgo will conservatively and carefully plan what they are going to acquire. They treat investments in the same way. They avoid get-rich-quick schemes and are very cautious about investing in stocks and shares, analysing the market accordingly. Indeed, their guiding principle seems to be: "If it's too good to be true, it probably is". This austerity is not due to meanness; rather it is due to the Virgoan's practical nature.

YOUR EDUCATION

Virgos take their education very seriously. They have a dream and they understand instinctively that through knowledge they can achieve their dream. They approach their education in a very practical way; they are not simply interested in knowledge for knowledge's sake but as a means to an end. Whatever career they decide upon they will get the qualifications that are required to enable them to do the job. Indeed they measure themselves by what they do rather than what they are. Virgoans look to achieve qualifications in a specialised manner. For example, if they study accountancy they will focus on a specific aspect of it.

Virgo – the Sun Sign

Above: Virgoans look to achieve qualifications in a specialised manner. For example, if they study accountancy they will focus on a specific aspect of it.

Virgo – the Sun Sign

YOUR CAREER AND AMBITIONS

Virgoans usually shine in any form of career which gives service to the general public: publishing, medicine and pharmaceuticals, accounting, secretarial work and nutrition. All these careers appeal to the Virgo's need to concentrate on detail and achieve perfection in what they do. There is very little that escapes their attention and, because of this, other suitable careers might be in investigative work or the Inland Revenue. They are good at working without supervision because they are extremely ethical and totally responsible. They often prefer to work quietly and alone; any job that allows for analysis is going to appeal to them. They do not make good promoters or advertisers of products as they are too honest to gloss over the deficiencies of any product they might sell.

They like working with modern and efficient equipment. The computer seems to have been invented for them as it is so much like them – Virgoans are human calculators. They are very good at focusing upon detailed aspects of their chosen career path.

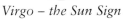

Virgo – the Sun Sign

Above: Virgoans like working with modern and efficient equipment. The computer seems to have been invented for them as it is so much like them.

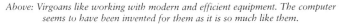

Virgo – the Sun Sign

YOUR FRIENDS

Virgoans tend to be loners at times. Indeed, like the Tarot card that represents Virgo, they are often hermits. Somewhere remote and quiet is their preferred location.

They rarely lavish affection upon their friends, but they are honest, steadfast and loyal once they have made friends, although they can be highly critical at times. They have a habit of cleaning up at their friends' houses, even if it is unnecessary. At parties, rather than being the life and soul, they can be found ensuring that everything gets washed up at the end.

They are sticklers for punctuality and if they make an appointment for a social engagement they will be there exactly on time and expect everyone else to do likewise. If they do join a group, they will spend their time analysing and discussing in great detail whatever the subject may be. They are ideal "trainspotters".

Above: Virgoans tend to be loners at times.

Virgo – the Sun Sign

YOUR HOPES AND FEARS

They fear dirt, untidiness, vulgarity, sloppiness and idleness as they believe that these lead to illness which is in fact their greatest fear. They hope that they can make their world a cleaner and more efficient place for everyone to live in.

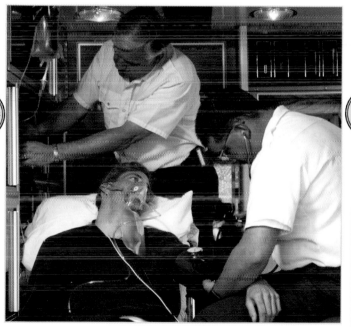

Above: illness is a Virgoan's greatest fear.

THE 12
MOON SIGNS

*To find out your moon sign either consult a professional astrologer or go to
my website www.jamespetulengro.co.uk for a free birth chart.*

ARIES

An Aries Moon means that you are extremely assertive in your nature on a subconscious level. Through the influence of Mars, life to you is one big adventure, with your ego ruling your feelings. You may come across as pushy because of your continual drive for success and your high self-motivation. You are very open to new ideas and concepts and can make quick decisions based on your instincts. It is rare that you use reasoning skills, preferring instead to leap into action. You often lose your temper over the smallest thing without a thought for the consequences. What you are thinking gets said as your mind is always active and

your emotions explode out of you, often before you have thought things through.

You are a bit of a rogue at times, with a "joie de vivre" which attracts many people to you. You are emotionally independent and will develop detachment from the people around you except perhaps from your immediate loved ones whom you will put on a pedestal. You feel with your ego.

Advice is something that you rarely take, preferring instead to rely on your own instincts. If someone gives you advice when it is not asked for, you can fly off the handle very quickly. The Moon in Aries can indicate a sense of

insecurity behind your independent and assertive exterior. You love challenges, particularly from a worthy opponent, but react emotionally when you lose. You rarely compromise, particularly when it comes to your feelings. However, when it comes to romance someone who can stand up to you will earn your respect.

At home you have an enthusiasm for DIY but you need to be in control of both the design and the work. This can often lead to domestic disputes.

TAURUS

A Taurus Moon means that you place great emphasis on material possessions. Your emotions are focused on getting the best that life has to offer. In terms of comfort, you cannot go without all of life's luxuries. You enjoy making your home environment beautiful and tasteful. You have a great love of collecting things, including people, and you can be extremely possessive about your friends and lovers. Emotionally you are very down-to-earth and practical and spend your time working to achieve your material desires in order to lead the good life that you feel you deserve. You have a natural business sense and can be very successful in the world of finance. The Moon is very stable in this sign as your emotional responses are slow but well thought out.

The 12 Moon Signs

As a friend you are good-natured, loyal and easygoing. You rarely lose your temper but, when you do, you can be very formidable. You would rather love than fight and can be very surprised at other people's rages. Small grievances rarely bother you. You have strong physical appetites and a deep emotional need to gratify them. You are very determined but sometimes stubborn and self indulgent, particularly for the good things in life.

You are a sensual and affectionate lover, and highly sexed, but you have a tendency to be over-possessive as you have a strong sense of ownership with both things and people. Your voice is pleasantly harmonious to others and you may well love singing and dancing and the arts in general as Taurus is ruled by Venus, the goddess of beauty.

You are generally very conservative in your outlook and, once you have decided what is true about life, you will stick to it and find change of any kind difficult. You must avoid becoming too narrow-minded in your opinions.

GEMINI

A Gemini Moon makes you witty and articulate with a tendency to feel with your mind. You are adaptable in your ideas and very attracted to mental stimulation. You enjoy socialising and the sign of the twins indicates a happy and easygoing personality. Your trademark is observation and you have a great gift for verbalising all of your ideas. You are friendly and gregarious and will have many friends, lovers and acquaintances. You truly love people of all kinds and, being ruled by Mercury, the messenger god, communication is your whole life. You are never at a loss for words but sometimes you can get carried away and end up arguing with yourself, both in your own mind and in conversations and debates. This sometimes confuses people as to what you really believe, as you can change your mind as quickly as you can change your clothes. In fact, you are likely to do both several times during a day.

The 12 Moon Signs

Your moods can be very changeable, up one moment and down the next, and you tend to be nervous in your movements. Some people may think you are shallow but actually you are torn apart by constantly changing feelings.

Your restless nature is always searching for new stimuli. Although you may not do too well academically you are a life-long student of knowledge itself and, like a butterfly, your mind will flit from subject to subject taking sustenance from each.

You have a great sense of humour and will be very entertaining at parties, although sometimes you can seem too cynical for some people and you can hurt people with cutting remarks which you will forget as quickly as you said them.

You are romantically inclined but in an intellectual way. You are fascinated more by the mind of your lovers than by their bodies. You are not the most faithful of the signs as you are always looking for something or someone better around the next corner. You are not the domestic type as you are moving around too much to settle down, until perhaps much later in life. You do not like to be tied down to one person or one place; freedom is important to you and you hate being restricted by emotional attachments.

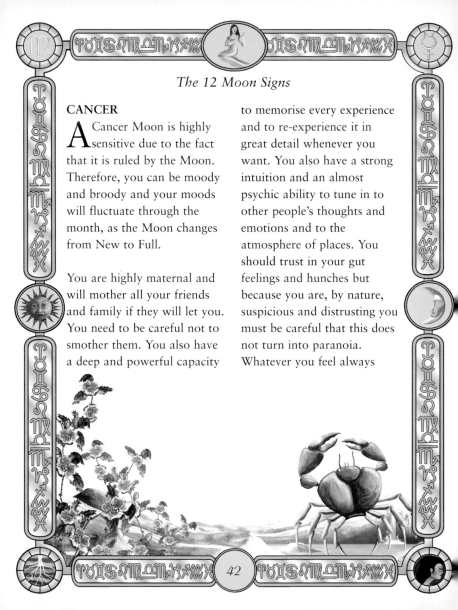

CANCER

A Cancer Moon is highly sensitive due to the fact that it is ruled by the Moon. Therefore, you can be moody and broody and your moods will fluctuate through the month, as the Moon changes from New to Full.

You are highly maternal and will mother all your friends and family if they will let you. You need to be careful not to smother them. You also have a deep and powerful capacity to memorise every experience and to re-experience it in great detail whenever you want. You also have a strong intuition and an almost psychic ability to tune in to other people's thoughts and emotions and to the atmosphere of places. You should trust in your gut feelings and hunches but because you are, by nature, suspicious and distrusting you must be careful that this does not turn into paranoia. Whatever you feel always

The 12 Moon Signs

all that is feminine in life. You have a great love of home and family which you will protect with your life. Of all the signs you are the greatest homemaker. Your domestic life needs to be safe and secure as this is the shell into which the crab that you are will retreat when disturbed. Some people only see your hard outer shell and forget that inside you are soft and kind.

remember that the Moon is affecting it. You go through cycles of feeling more than any other sign. You must be careful not to mistake your feelings for the feelings of the people around you that you are picking up on.

You are gentle, peaceful and romantic and appreciative of

You are particularly interested in history and your ancestors, and Cancer Moons love their country. You need to feel that you are in control of the whole world and can become withdrawn and ill when you lose control of any part of it. Change is not something that you relish.

Above: of all the signs you are the greatest homemaker. Your domestic life needs to be safe and secure.

LEO

Leo Moons have a sunny disposition and a desire to lead in all walks of life. You are generally confident, cheerful and optimistic. Emotionally you are happy-go-lucky and hedonistic. You are self-sufficient and self-reliant, and deeply emotionally involved in all undertakings. You love display and pageants, especially if you are personally involved in them. This may lead you to being involved in drama, whether on the stage or in the home. You feel that you can do anything that you want and your creative ability feels as though it has no bounds. You may appear to others to be haughty and somewhat spoilt. This is because you have a tendency to think of yourself as royalty and the rest of humanity as your subjects. You have a need to be admired and even applauded and you are constantly seeking appreciation and attention. You have a natural creative flair in the home with a gift for interior design, and your

The 12 Moon Signs

surroundings will always be flamboyant and probably expensive. You think of your home as your palace and, in seeking to impress others, you may well overspend at times. You are a social climber and demand respect from all those around you. You are straightforward and usually dignified, enabling you to gain responsibility and status. Nothing hurts you more than when you feel unappreciated and your pride has been stepped upon. You have a natural nobility but you can be egocentric and even pompous. It is very difficult for you to back down or accept any sort of compromise – after all you are the Ruler.

You are a loving and devoted parent and will cosset and play with your children with great affection and warmth. You love giving and have a great sense of charity towards those worse off than you. You are highly emotional with a strong drive for power and prominence.

Above: you are a loving and devoted parent and will cosset and play with your children with great affection and warmth.

VIRGO

Virgo Moons are reserved, analytical and critical. You may seem unemotional to others as it is difficult for you to express what you feel. Consequently, you can come across as cold and detached and sometimes even prudish and stuffy, when in fact you are highly emotional and easily hurt.

You may have a deep-seated inferiority complex which may lead you to proving yourself through your intellectual superiority. You always consider the practical application of study rather than just learning for its own sake.

You are generally shy and so you respond well to encouragement and appreciation, although you rarely give this to others. You are your own worst enemy and assume that because you are over-critical of yourself that others do the same. You have very little in the way of self-esteem. You may feel that people don't like you, for this

is a placement that shows much lack of self-esteem, thus you tend to be emotionally reserved. Your talents lie in expressing your feelings through writing and poetry as your Moon is ruled by Mercury, the messenger god. Consequently you will be ruled by your mind rather than by your heart and you will have trouble understanding highly emotional and passionate people. Your reactions often seem detached and rather cold. Self-analysis may occupy a lot of your thoughts and in fact psychoanalysis and psychiatry would be good careers for you.

You are too introverted to have a strong sex drive and you will be shy about the physical act and have

difficulty in accepting its undignified side. Within a relationship you will attempt to make yourself indispensable to your partner, thereby securing your love, and you respond well to responsibility. In the home you are particularly concerned with hygiene, health and diet and will be constantly involved in tidying up and cleaning.

Virgo Moon is an earthy moon so you are practical and have a definite sense of the realities of life. You are at your best when you are taking care of someone who is in need of you. You can be temperamental and argumentative, but you have a shrewd business sense and pay meticulous attention to detail.

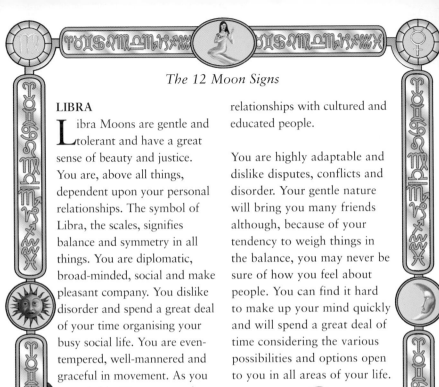

LIBRA

Libra Moons are gentle and tolerant and have a great sense of beauty and justice. You are, above all things, dependent upon your personal relationships. The symbol of Libra, the scales, signifies balance and symmetry in all things. You are diplomatic, broad-minded, social and make pleasant company. You dislike disorder and spend a great deal of your time organising your busy social life. You are even-tempered, well-mannered and graceful in movement. As you are ruled by Venus, art and beauty are paramount in your life, as is your search for the perfect partner. You cannot bear coarseness or vulgarity and will seek relationships with cultured and educated people.

You are highly adaptable and dislike disputes, conflicts and disorder. Your gentle nature will bring you many friends although, because of your tendency to weigh things in the balance, you may never be sure of how you feel about people. You can find it hard to make up your mind quickly and will spend a great deal of time considering the various possibilities and options open to you in all areas of your life.

The 12 Moon Signs

Your home, which is very important to you, will be harmonious and tranquil and full of beautiful objects. You are particularly attracted towards the arts and may make a career in this direction. Anything that you can make more beautiful will be given a makeover, including people.

You enjoy the company of people and do not like to spend much time alone. You need to be liked and your emotional well-being depends on being appreciated for the beautiful person that you really are, for you truly are a thoughtful and good-natured person who will go out of their way to be kind to others. At many times in your life you will seem to be in crisis and have difficulty in making decisions because you are capable of seeing both sides equally. As often as not your decision will be based on the toss of a coin. You can sometimes be too willing to compromise and frequently allow others to take advantage of you in the name of peace and because it is easier to let other people make decisions. For your partner you can be self-sacrificing and happy to fulfil his or her needs before your own.

A solid, steady relationship is your preference. You love to receive small gifts and you are a romantic at heart. You do your best to spread beauty and harmony wherever you can.

SCORPIO

Scorpio Moons are the most passionate and secretive of all the signs. You are highly sensitive and have an uncanny memory which leads you to remember both pleasant and unpleasant memories which can sometimes leave deep psychic scars. You enjoy life to the full and have an innate understanding that through suffering character is formed. You are the most sexual of all signs, but you combine your sexuality with deep spirituality.

Pluto, the ruler of the underworld, can lead you into the depths of your unconscious where you may find disturbing feelings but, having entered into your underworld, you return strangely refreshed and born anew. You have a great capacity for regeneration and will die many times in your lifetime. Change is what you thrive on. You need to learn to come to terms with your deep emotions as other signs are not as emotionally intense as you. You may find that

The 12 Moon Signs

you see other people as shallow. Your real nature is not apparent to others as, until you get to know somebody deeply, you tend to hide your true feelings. But once you love, you love passionately and the object of your affection can take over your whole existence. This can also be so for your children as you will bestow an all-consuming love upon them. You are a good homemaker, provided that you get your own way in it, but you prefer the company of your immediate family rather than entertaining all and sundry.

In all your relationships you are extremely possessive and jealous and can even become violent when your passions are thwarted. No-one says "no" to a Scorpio Moon. You can be domineering and will often use your sexual favours to get what you want. You have a problem with judging people too quickly and, if they make a mistake, you rarely give them a second chance. You react to emotional situations in an abrupt and impulsive way. You can also be vindictive, spiteful and vengeful when wronged and are easily hurt. You are very determined in achieving your ambitions and thrive on new challenges. You are an extremist by nature and never pursue anything light-heartedly; even when a situation becomes detrimental you insist on seeing it through to the end.

SAGITTARIUS

A Sagittarius Moon indicates feelings of restlessness which requires a great deal of physical activity in order to disperse pent-up emotion. You need your freedom to wander where and when you will. You are happy-go-lucky, enthusiastic and highly optimistic and at your best when you are mobile. Because of your eternal optimism you can be socially naïve and blissfully unaware of social differences. This can sometimes make you socially inept because you tend to see all people as equals. You have high ideals and meet people on your own terms by melting and merging into relationships with them like a friendly puppy does. You are generally good-natured, fun loving and jovial like Jupiter that rules this sign. You always know who you are and where you are heading, but

The 12 Moon Signs

are adaptable enough to change direction when it feels that you will learn more.

Learning is very important to you, although you have a tendency not to learn from your mistakes. The learning that you are interested in is the knowledge of all things, particularly the mysteries of the universe. You make a fine teacher or spiritual adviser.

Your home may not be tidy but will be filled with objects that you have gathered on your travels. You will be very enthusiastic in teaching your children everything they want to know and encouraging them to expand their knowledge whenever you can, being more of a friend than a parent.

It is important to you that your partners are also your friends as well as your lovers. You display your affections openly and need a partner who will play, socialise and travel places with you without making too many demands. Being free and without restraints is one of your deepest needs.

Sporting activities will help keep your weight down as you have a predisposition to over-indulge in eating and drinking.

You are prone to many changes in your life, particularly to changes of residence or career which you need to fulfil your restless nature.

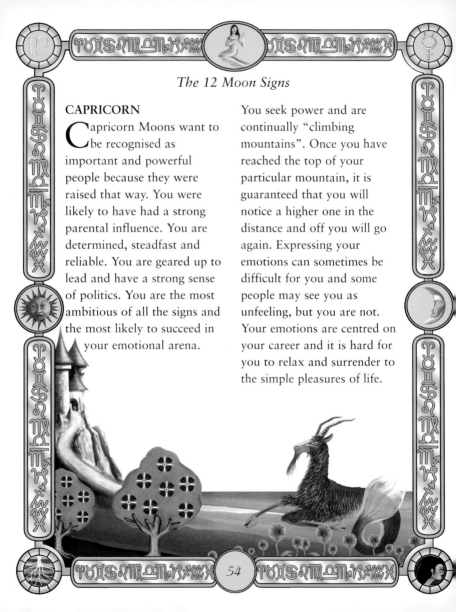

CAPRICORN

Capricorn Moons want to be recognised as important and powerful people because they were raised that way. You were likely to have had a strong parental influence. You are determined, steadfast and reliable. You are geared up to lead and have a strong sense of politics. You are the most ambitious of all the signs and the most likely to succeed in your emotional arena.

You seek power and are continually "climbing mountains". Once you have reached the top of your particular mountain, it is guaranteed that you will notice a higher one in the distance and off you will go again. Expressing your emotions can sometimes be difficult for you and some people may see you as unfeeling, but you are not. Your emotions are centred on your career and it is hard for you to relax and surrender to the simple pleasures of life.

The 12 Moon Signs

You are the parent of the Zodiac because you are ruled by Saturn, the god of time. Because of this, you are likely to seem old when you are young and young when you are old. Some Moon in Capricorns have a Peter Pan complex but only inside; on the outside they appear to be wise beyond their years. Whatever your goals are you will strive to achieve them, stubbornly and persistently. You are a very hard worker and will take on goals that would frighten other signs.

You are conservative in your emotions, not in a political sense, but in a true sense of conservation. This is your way – not to create new things but to improve upon and conserve what has come before you. If you are thwarted in your goals, you can become despondent and moody and begin to look at the negative side of things. You need to develop a more optimistic approach to life. Capricorn Moons can be shy but have a very clever sense of humour and can lead people to do what they want with this humour.

Your home life, like your career, will be ambitious. You will want to live in the best house in the best part of town. A Capricorn Moon loves renovating old property and your taste is normally classical. A lot of Capricorn Moons work from home due to their tendency to be shy

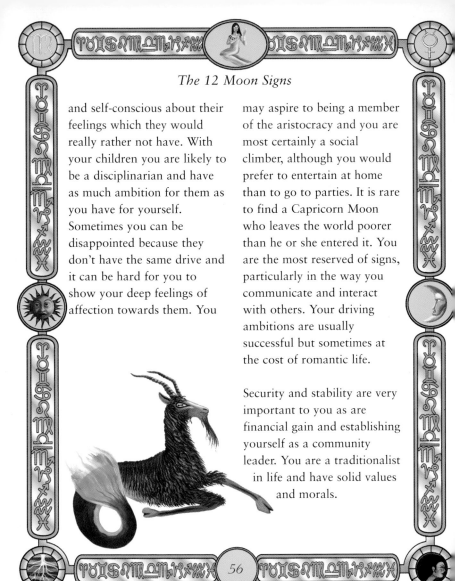

and self-conscious about their feelings which they would really rather not have. With your children you are likely to be a disciplinarian and have as much ambition for them as you have for yourself. Sometimes you can be disappointed because they don't have the same drive and it can be hard for you to show your deep feelings of affection towards them. You may aspire to being a member of the aristocracy and you are most certainly a social climber, although you would prefer to entertain at home than to go to parties. It is rare to find a Capricorn Moon who leaves the world poorer than he or she entered it. You are the most reserved of signs, particularly in the way you communicate and interact with others. Your driving ambitions are usually successful but sometimes at the cost of romantic life.

Security and stability are very important to you as are financial gain and establishing yourself as a community leader. You are a traditionalist in life and have solid values and morals.

The 12 Moon Signs

AQUARIUS

Aquarius Moons produce the most modern and progressive people of all the signs. However, you can sometimes be erratic in some of the ideals you hold. You are unusual and unpredictable, with a broad imagination. You are most likely to engage in many kinds of group activities and have a wide range of friends from all walks of life. You have a capacity to see inside people and not be taken in by appearances. For you a beggar may be an angel in disguise.

You have a very creative imagination and your many friends will value your input into their lives. Sometimes your high ideals can get in the way of practicality and common sense. You have a quality that puts you ahead of your time and some people may see you as downright eccentric. You are attracted to all things that are modern and innovative as you are ruled by Uranus, the god of change. You love the sciences and would dearly love to invent something to improve the lot of humanity.

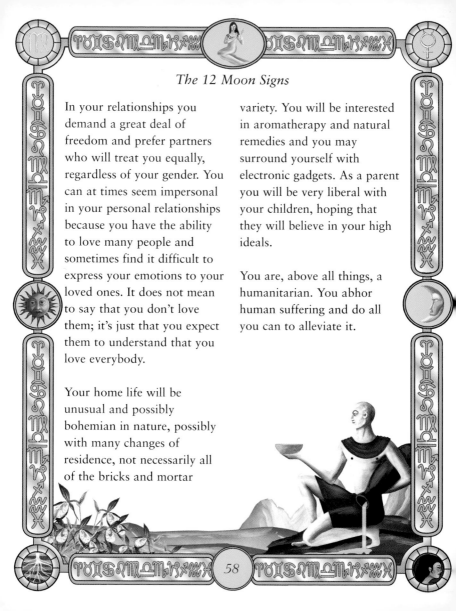

The 12 Moon Signs

In your relationships you demand a great deal of freedom and prefer partners who will treat you equally, regardless of your gender. You can at times seem impersonal in your personal relationships because you have the ability to love many people and sometimes find it difficult to express your emotions to your loved ones. It does not mean to say that you don't love them; it's just that you expect them to understand that you love everybody.

Your home life will be unusual and possibly bohemian in nature, possibly with many changes of residence, not necessarily all of the bricks and mortar

variety. You will be interested in aromatherapy and natural remedies and you may surround yourself with electronic gadgets. As a parent you will be very liberal with your children, hoping that they will believe in your high ideals.

You are, above all things, a humanitarian. You abhor human suffering and do all you can to alleviate it.

The 12 Moon Signs

PISCES

A Moon in Pisces means that you have a great understanding of what it is to be human, albeit in a somewhat dreamy sense. You are gifted with great sensitivity and perception, allowing you to have great compassion and consideration for other people. This Moon means you have great empathy towards others in a psychic way and you often experience their emotions.

Since Neptune, the god of the sea rules your Moon, you need to ensure that you are not flooded by people's moods and desires psychically. Therefore you should meditate and reflect on your own feelings in solitude.

Life to you is permanently rose-tinted, no matter how harsh the reality. Everyone's "little faults" are ignored, no matter how big.

At times, though, your over-optimism, and unselfishness can leave you open to others taking advantage of your passive nature. Your misplaced trust means that you often end up hurt and feeling sorry for yourself. Rather than blame the other person, you tend to turn in on

yourself, again resulting in melancholy.

You will spend a great deal of your time searching for answers to life's great questions and will read a great many books on a wide variety of subjects. At times you will seek a more spiritual way of life. You are surprisingly ambitious and, because of your gift of creative visualisation, you can achieve your goals. However, you do not have the competitive drive of other signs and so can lack self-confidence.

Trust is something that you do not give freely. When you are entirely comfortable with someone you can then be surprisingly bossy as this is your way of showing that you trust them. In marriage you are so supportive that you are in danger of becoming a martyr. You need love and approval and, although you are happy to live alone, you prefer to give and receive love. Sometimes you can be so shy and repressed that you do not find the love you require

The 12 Moon Signs

and instead retreat into yourself. As a parent you empathise with your children but prefer those that can actively respond rather than young babies.

You are incredibly romantic and love all the little things which make up a relationship. Sex is something you enjoy as it combines all your favourite feelings and sensations.

Your home is your haven, a place where you can withdraw from the hustle and bustle of everyday life. However, you will also have many friends and visitors coming and going, particularly as you rarely lock your doors. People are drawn to you because they know

that you are a good shoulder to cry on and will assist as much as possible with their personal problems. You need to ensure, however, that you do not sacrifice yourself for others too much.

Above: you are incredibly romantic and love all the little things which make up a relationship.

VIRGO SUN
AND THE 12 MOON SIGN COMBINATIONS

When you calculate a birth chart you will discover that the Moon as well as the planets will sometimes be in different signs of the Zodiac. The whole chart gives the whole picture of the personality, but the Sun and the Moon have the most powerful effect upon us. When you combine the Sun sign and the Moon sign you are combining different parts of the Zodiac. Some signs work well together and some signs don't, in the same way that two Sun signs may live in eternal conflict where others live in harmony; so it is with the Sun and Moon in your chart. What follows is an explanation of the combinations between your Virgo Sun and various other moons that may appear in your birth chart.

VIRGO SUN AND ARIES MOON

The combination of your earthy Sun and fiery Moon sign is a difficult one as the signs conflict with each other. The qualities that the signs have in common are hardness combined with an aggressive strength of purpose. You will rarely show your emotions. Your personality will be high-spirited, combative and

Virgo Sun and the 12 Moon Sign Combinations

critical with a high degree of nervous tension. You are not sociable by nature because you are so critical of other people's beliefs and actions. You do, however, manage to hold onto friends because of your honesty and directness.

You are always exacting and demanding, and whatever task you choose to undertake you will pursue it until you decide it is perfect. Although you have an air of self-confidence about you, it is actually covering up a hidden inferiority complex. In executive positions, you will rarely be a popular figure but you will always get the job done. Your mental processes are careful and accurate and you always think before you

act. You not only have a sharp mind but you have a sharp tongue and you need to learn not to be so hard on people. You have great insights into other people's natures. However, you do have difficulty in being objective about yourself because of your lack of emotion which is not good for self-appraisal. You will express emotion on some occasions but only when it serves your purpose. These emotions are not often truly felt. You generally view emotion and sentimentality as character weaknesses and you find others who exhibit such traits repellent. Your speedy mental processes and ambition allow you to succeed in any career path

that you choose. Writing, in particular, is a form of self-expression that you could excel in because of your detachment.

VIRGO SUN AND TAURUS MOON

The double combination of your earthy Sun sign and earthy Moon sign makes you a sensible, sturdy and reliable personality. This combination often brings material success and wealth. Even though your life is likely to be fortunate, you will still worry a great deal and often lose your confidence in getting projects off the ground. Your friendly personality and sharp mind are the keys to your success. Security is always very important to you, as are your roots. Although you are the salt-of-the-earth type you are also highly strung because of the mutable nature of Virgo. You need time to think things through and your sharp mind will always find a solution to any problem that may occur. There is nothing eccentric or unconventional about you and, although you are not highly ambitious, the good things of life seem to naturally flow in your direction.

You have the capacity to work hard and stick with any job until it is finished. It is rare for you to initiate projects, but you are excellent at overseeing and helping other people to realise their dreams. You would make a good sergeant major because you have a very direct way of dealing with people and do not beat about the bush. Even if you were not naturally born into a fortunate environment, you will soon create one for yourself and your family through your great common sense and practicality. Farming, gardening and cooking are all areas that you could excel in as you have a natural feel for them.

VIRGO SUN AND GEMINI MOON

The combination of your earthy Sun and airy Moon signs, both ruled by the planet Mercury, gives you great strength of mind. Your reasoning is fast and brilliant. You are capable of figuring things out analytically and rationally, particularly intricate and detailed problems. You live mainly in your mind and, because of this, your emotions are usually underdeveloped. You tend to act with cold logic in most situations. You are able to detect the underlying motives of others, but your responses to these perceptions are rarely sympathetic or emotional. You have great

Virgo Sun and the 12 Moon Sign Combinations

difficulty in integrating feelings and logic. Your great thirst for knowledge makes you a natural and eternal student and your aptitude for detailed work alongside abstract and philosophical thought could lead you into an academic career. To some people you may appear too changeable and fickle, but this is because you are interested in a variety of subjects.

Because you spend so much time involved with mental processes, you may not pay attention to your physical well-being which could lead you into health problems. You need to make particular efforts to keep your body in shape. Although you will usually criticise any health regimes that

are available, because of their lack of logic, you need to watch your diet and get plenty of physical exercise. However, it is unlikely that you will ever get fat because you have so much nervous energy running through you which burns up calories, but your muscle tone may deteriorate in time. In your youth active sport may be important to you but as you grow older you will retreat more and more into your mind. All of your interests are likely to be passive or intellectual in nature. Exercise is your best medicine.

You will excel in any career associated with the mental processes, particularly journalism or computer software design.

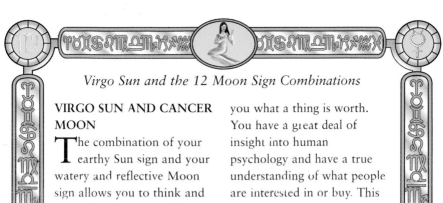

Virgo Sun and the 12 Moon Sign Combinations

VIRGO SUN AND CANCER MOON

The combination of your earthy Sun sign and your watery and reflective Moon sign allows you to think and feel with great depth. The analytical and discriminatory aspect of Virgo blends well with the sensitive intuition of Cancer. You are greatly influenced by environmental conditions and other people that you come into contact with. Although you appear to be changeable on the outside, on the inside you are practical. Your intuitive insight into detail often allows you to know the truth of any issue that you are presented with. Your good sense of value will always tell you what a thing is worth. You have a great deal of insight into human psychology and have a true understanding of what people are interested in or buy. This allows you to progress in any business opportunities that you may choose. You have protective and defensive instincts towards your family and they mean a great deal to you. At times you can be over-fussy with them.

Although you form close attachments to the people around you, you are usually cautious and reserved with strangers and it takes a great deal of time for them to gain your trust. You are conservative and traditional in your habits. You find all

changes difficult and, if you have to accept them, it takes you a long time. Your innate understanding of human nature would suggest that a career in psychology or counselling, especially of women, would suit you. Also, working with food, nutrition and children would use your talents to the full.

VIRGO SUN AND LEO MOON

The combination of your earthy Sun and fiery Moon signs produces a very sincere, confident and vital personality. At times you can come across as an authoritative figure. You are conscientious and have a great capacity for devotion and duty to work. However, your assertive impulses may sometimes become aggressive, giving rise to a tendency to worry about what you might have said or done at a later date. You always feel better when you are not pushed into making rash decisions. You have strong beliefs and principles and you expect

Above: working with food and nutrition would use your talents to the full.

Virgo Sun and the 12 Moon Sign Combinations

others to recognise and hold to these; your close friends usually do. You are discriminating and practical and your strength of character and strict ethics should gain you a high position in life. You should be aware of taking too long a time over decision-making as you could end up vacillating. You do have a great deal of physical vitality as well as intellectual power. A career as a teacher, particularly with children, would suit you. You could also be drawn to the world of theatre and drama, maybe as a scriptwriter or director. You are particularly adroit at carrying out detailed tasks to their conclusion and are able to inspire others to do the same.

VIRGO SUN AND VIRGO MOON

You were born around the time of the New Moon with both your Sun and your Moon sign in earthy Virgo. Your life will be dominated by intellectual pursuits. You can be finicky and fussy in your tastes, particularly with dress, food and in your home. This will make you very conventional in your outlook. You look for relationships where there is a mental affinity rather than a physical or romantic one. Your natural aloofness will prevent you from getting involved with anyone who, in your opinion, has an inferior mind. Because

Virgo Sun and the 12 Moon Sign Combinations

of your perfectionist nature you will have difficulty finding like-minded individuals. You rarely take risks and you dislike anything radical or eccentric. You have a great ability to focus and stay on one course in order to achieve your aims. These aims will be inherently practical as you are constantly seeking security in the real world.

You are not easily convinced by smooth-talking people because of your powers of discrimination. You believe in preserving the status quo and, even though you recognise that improvements are needed in society, you want them to occur in an orderly, well-thought out way. One of the things that is really important to you is a peaceful life; you do not have a

Above: one of the things that is really important to you is a peaceful life.

revolutionary spirit. For you gradual change is the best way forward. You do hold tightly onto your ideas but equally you are able to understand and appreciate the ideas of others. Sometimes your decisions can be hard to plan and execute. You have a great many theories that you would like to try out but you know that only the practicalities of life are worth pursuing. You are a perfectionist with a keen sense of duty and you demand a great deal from yourself. This often stems from an unhappy childhood or underlying health issues.

A career that enables you to use your talent in analysing fine detail, such as laboratory research, would suit you best.

VIRGO SUN AND LIBRA MOON

The combination of your earthy Sun sign and your airy Moon sign produces a personality that is harmonious and well balanced. You are able to use your intelligence to make careful and informed judgements. You are generally a friendly person, but you have the ability to remain detached and impersonal in your relationships. Your self-restraint prevents you from ever becoming overbearing in any situation. You rarely give an opinion unless you have something valuable to offer and, even then, only when your are persuaded. You

Virgo Sun and the 12 Moon Sign Combinations

enjoy the quiet life. Extremes are not for you and the companions that you choose will be of a similar nature. The critical side of Virgo is softened by the Venusian aspect of Libra so, although you may think critically about a person's actions, you rarely say anything that will hurt or offend them. You hate coarseness and vulgarity. You are, however, a lover of humanity but many people find you aloof and difficult to get to know. You do not suffer fools gladly. You will lead a peaceful and unassuming life without interfering with others. You tread the path of life lightly. The Moon in Libra indicates that you enjoy friendships but not on a deep level, so you

are likely to have many acquaintances but few close friends. Because you are curious and love to experiment and have a talent for mental analysis and impartial judgements, the law, as a career, would suit you or medical research.

Above: the law, as a career, would suit you or medical research.

VIRGO SUN AND SCORPIO MOON

The combination of your earthy Sun and your watery but fixed Moon sign produces an individual who appears to be a thoughtful intellectual but who is really driven by their emotions. This is the most emotional combination of all Virgoans. Your Scorpio lunar nature indicates a rash and impulsive nature, tempered by the common sense of Virgo.

Your ability to reason and rationalise is highly developed but sometimes you find it difficult to believe ideas that affect you emotionally. You become very partisan in whatever causes that you take up. You may be drawn to religious or spiritual groups but you try to approach these with your intellect. You are very persuasive at putting your ideas across and have a brilliant intellectual capacity that, at times, seems like genius. At other times your emotions get in the way and you miss the point completely. You are a theoretical and radical thinker, able to prove almost everything on paper with diagrams but whether it works in practice is another thing entirely. Your intellectual powers are very strong but not often realistic. You are a zealous person which makes it hard for you to listen to what others have

Virgo Sun and the 12 Moon Sign Combinations

to say and you can be dominating when you are working with groups of people. Underneath all this is a deep, brooding personality that is forever searching for ideas which you can either espouse or dismiss. You are likely to be very successful in business and valuable to any employer because you possess strong leadership qualities. Nevertheless, you need to learn to curb your emotional outbursts and, if you do so, you will find your life and your relationships much easier to handle. Any work in the medical profession would suit you. You have a particular talent for spiritual healing and mediumship. You may also be attracted to the religious life and perhaps would be suited to living in a religious or spiritual community.

Above: any work in the medical profession would suit you.

VIRGO SUN AND SAGITTARIUS MOON

The combination of your earthy Sun sign and fiery Moon sign indicates a personality that spends much of its time thinking about travelling or doing great deeds but the analytical aspect of Virgo often puts a damper on these dreams. You are also capable of doing things that other people disapprove of, for the sake of adventure, romance and excitement. The puritanical nature of the Virgin may be suppressed in order for you to accumulate the experiences in life that you so desire. You are not a classic Virgo. Many of the thoughts that run through your head are not based in the real world. You are philosophical and introspective, but you rarely look deeply inside yourself.

You are highly idealistic and at times other people will find it hard to meet your expectations. You spend a great deal of your life day-dreaming, and if you can realise your dreams you are very creative. The challenge in your life will be to control your restless mind and concentrate on working with things close at hand. You are likely to have a talent for acting and can be very dramatic in your social life. You are particularly clever at communicating through body language. However, you do have a tendency towards bluntness in dealing with

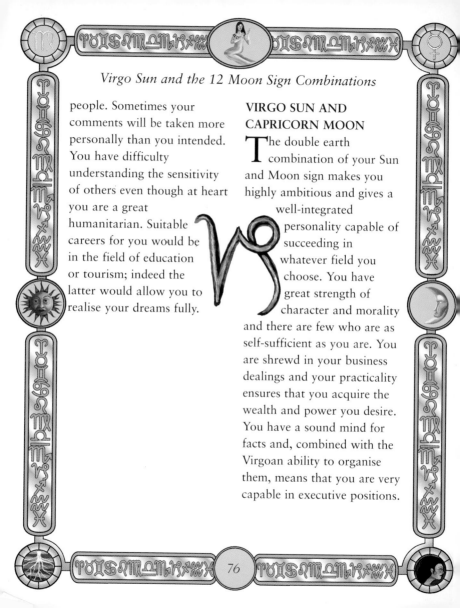

people. Sometimes your comments will be taken more personally than you intended. You have difficulty understanding the sensitivity of others even though at heart you are a great humanitarian. Suitable careers for you would be in the field of education or tourism; indeed the latter would allow you to realise your dreams fully.

VIRGO SUN AND CAPRICORN MOON

The double earth combination of your Sun and Moon sign makes you highly ambitious and gives a well-integrated personality capable of succeeding in whatever field you choose. You have great strength of character and morality and there are few who are as self-sufficient as you are. You are shrewd in your business dealings and your practicality ensures that you acquire the wealth and power you desire. You have a sound mind for facts and, combined with the Virgoan ability to organise them, means that you are very capable in executive positions.

Virgo Sun and the 12 Moon Sign Combinations

You value your independence and dislike being beholden to others.

You have a reputation for being trustworthy and having a high level of personal integrity. At times your dedication and seriousness can lead you to miss out on the fun parts of life. You are extremely devoted to your family, but you need to remember to give more time to them. If you set your goals high then you are very capable of achieving them.

**VIRGO SUN AND
AQUARIUS MOON**

The combination of your earthy Sun and airy Moon signs produces a personality that on the one hand is very practical and down-to-earth, but on the other hand is likely to spend time searching for cosmic truths, knowledge and understanding. You do strive to be above the mundane elements of everyday life. This combination of signs has little time for human emotion or passion. You are inclined to be cool and self-sufficient and can sometimes be insensitive in the way that you deal with people. You are not known for your diplomacy or tact and usually tell people what

  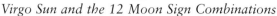

Virgo Sun and the 12 Moon Sign Combinations

you believe is right, rather than what they want to hear. You are objective in the extreme although this does not mean you are incapable of sympathy. However, you do not allow your judgement to become clouded with emotion. In your relationships it is more important for you to have an intellectual connection, rather than an emotional or physical one.

You can spend hours becoming absorbed in and occupied by the details of an idea or plan, particularly in politics or humanitarian and charity schemes. You have a great capacity for mental exploration, always scheming and dreaming and trying to satisfy your endless curiosity.

You can be somewhat suspicious and often too judgmental. Your mind is unconventional in its workings, but in the end you are always guided by your sound analytical and intuitive sense. A career in politics or within charitable institutions would suit you best. You would also make a good teacher.

Above: a career in politics or within charitable institutions would suit you best. You would also make a good teacher.

VIRGO SUN AND PISCES MOON

You were born around the time of the Full Moon and the combination of your earthy Sun sign with your polar opposite and watery Moon sign gives you a deep and profound personality. You are not only intellectual but intuitive as well. You have the ability to work things out with pure logic as well as using your feelings. You were born wise and seem to have an innate understanding of the workings of the universe. You have a great deal of emotional sensitivity which, blended with the analytical insight and discrimination of Virgo, sets you aside from most people. This strong blend of keen intellect and intuition may move you towards more dreamy pursuits, rather than earthy practical ones.

You are a good friend and listener. You are strongly empathic and seem to know instinctively what advice to give. However, you have to ensure that you do not get overwhelmed by the needs of others. If you do, you will find that you end up being too introspective in your analysis. The caring professions, the arts or work involving nutrition are best suited to you.

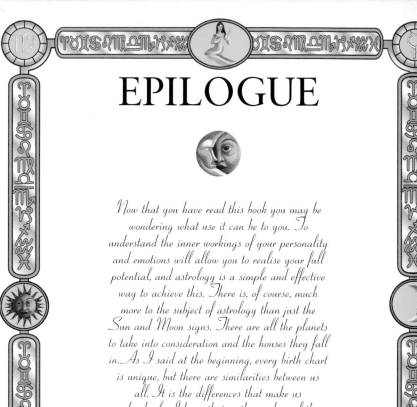

EPILOGUE

Now that you have read this book you may be wondering what use it can be to you. To understand the inner workings of your personality and emotions will allow you to realise your full potential, and astrology is a simple and effective way to achieve this. There is, of course, much more to the subject of astrology than just the Sun and Moon signs. There are all the planets to take into consideration and the houses they fall in. As I said at the beginning, every birth chart is unique, but there are similarities between us all. It is the differences that make us individuals. I hope that in the reading of this book perhaps you will be inspired to look deeper into yourself and deeper into the uses of astrology.

"Know yourself and the truth will set you free"